It's Magic!

Charlotte Raby

OXFORD
UNIVERSITY PRESS

OXFORD
UNIVERSITY PRESS

is a department of the University of Oxford.
It furthers the University's objective of excellence in research, scholarship, and education by publishing worldwide in

Oxford New York
Auckland Cape Town Dar es Salaam Hong Kong Karachi
Kuala Lumpur Madrid Melbourne Mexico City Nairobi
New Delhi Shanghai Taipei Toronto

With offices in

Argentina Austria Brazil Chile Czech Republic France Greece
Guatemala Hungary Italy Japan Poland Portugal Singapore
South Korea Switzerland Thailand Turkey Ukraine Vietnam

Oxford is a registered trade mark of Oxford University Press in the UK and in certain other countries

First published 2007

British Library Cataloguing in Publication Data

Data available

ISBN: 978-0-19-846106-7

9 10 8

Printed in China

Paper used in the production of this book is a natural, recyclable product made from wood grown in sustainable forests. The manufacturing process conforms to the environmental regulations of the country of origin

Acknowledgements

The publisher would like to thank the following for permission to reproduce photographs: **p4**t Photographers Direct/Ryan Howell, **p4**b Maartje van Caspel/iStockphoto; **p5** PA Photos; **p6** Visual Arts Library (London)/Alamy; **p7** Mary Evans Picture Library/Mary Evans Picture Library; **p8**bl Eric Ryan/Getty Images, **p8**br Eric Ryan/Getty Images, **p8**t B. Bird/Zefa/Corbis UK Ltd.; **p9**l Digital Vision/Getty Images, **p9**r Digital Vision/Getty Images; **p10**l Reuters/Corbis UK Ltd.; **p10**r The Houdini Museum, **p11**t The Houdini Museum, **p11**b Juliana Chen; **p12**t Scott Wintrow/Getty Images, **p12**b Jennifer Brown/Star Ledger/Corbis UK Ltd.; **p13**l Mitchell Gerber/Corbis UK Ltd., **p13**r Erik C Pendzich/Rex Features; **p15** Photographers Direct/Freezepic Photography; **p16**t NILS JORGENSEN/Rex Features, **p16**b Vista Photo Agency/Zakary Belamy; **p17**t John Turner/Corbis UK Ltd., **p17**b Natalia Bratslavsky/iStockphoto; **p21** Taryn Cass/Zooid Pictures

Additional photography by Chris Honeywell

Cover photograph: Getty/photographers choice

Illustrations by Carol Jonas: **p7**, **p22**; Sean Longcroft: **p14**, **p15**, **p20**

Contents

Note! *It's Magic!* contains descriptions of magic tricks as well as some stunts. **Only** the four tricks described in detail are suitable for children to perform. The other tricks and stunts are described for illustrative purposes only.

Introduction

Magic may be as old as humankind. Once it was used to explain strange natural happenings like earthquakes and floods. Now magic is seen as entertainment. We don't believe that magicians have special powers but we do believe they are skilled in tricking us.

We think, 'How did they do that?'

Magicians practise each trick until it is perfect. This is because they have taken the Magician's **Oath**, which means they have promised never to perform an **illusion** until it looks like magic.

In this book, there are four tricks you can perform. You can amaze and confuse your friends with your 'magical' skills. But be warned – if you really want to perform magic you must work hard. Wait until your trick looks like magic, then enjoy the praise your hard work deserves.

Performing magic must be a wonderful experience because many of the famous magicians began at an early age and never stopped!

Magic through the ages

Did you know?

The Greeks enjoyed street magic – especially rather gory tricks involving swords!

While Egyptian slaves built the pyramids they were entertained by a magician called Dedi. He made birds and other animals appear and vanish, and was the first known performer of the Cup and Balls trick.

The Conjuror, painted by the Dutch artist Hieronymus Bosch, in the 15th century, shows a magician performing the Cup and Balls trick.

The Chinese Linking Rings trick is believed to be the first-ever magic trick. It is still a very popular trick, which delights people today.

Medieval people enjoyed many of the same tricks as we do today at fairs. Even royalty enjoyed watching magic in medieval times.

In the 1840s in France, the first-ever magic theatre was opened by a man called Jean Robert-Houdin. He is considered to be the 'Father of Modern Magic'.

The magic seven

Magicians believe that there are only seven different types of magic trick. But what are they?

1. Production tricks

This is when 'something appears out of nothing'. If a magician finds an egg in your ear, it is a production illusion.

2. Vanishing tricks

A 'vanish' is the opposite of a production – a magician makes 'something become nothing'. For example, a coin or a person disappears.

3. Restoration tricks

These tricks are called restorations because they restore something back to its proper state. For example, a torn-up newspaper magically becomes whole.

4. Transformation tricks

These change one thing into something else. For example a card you are holding magically becomes a flower!

5. Teleportation

This is when the magician moves something from one place to another – invisibly. For example a watch 'disappears' and then later is found in a locked box.

6. Levitation illusions

If a magician makes something rise into the air it is a levitation trick. You can try a simple levitation illusion later in the book!

7. Penetration tricks

It is called a penetration when something solid seems to pass through another solid object.

Here are four solid steel hoops.

Hey presto! They are joined together! This is a penetration trick.

Four magicians

These four magicians have all been important people in the world of magic.

Harry Houdini is a very important name in magic. He invented his name to honour Jean Robert-Houdin. Harry was a famous **escapologist** and invented many tricks that are still performed today. The best known is the Chinese Water Torture trick. Houdini was held upside down in a locked glass and steel cabinet full of water, from which he escaped!

The Chinese Water Tourture trick

David Copperfield is famous for his vanishing tricks.The most incredible one he did was making the Statue of Liberty disappear. David makes magic on a huge scale, unlike anyone before him.

Dorothy Dietrich is a famous magician. She is the only woman to have caught a bullet in her teeth or escaped from a straightjacket whilst hanging from a burning rope. She is also well known for her production tricks – making coins appear from thin air.

Juliana Chen came to Canada from China and began to perform as a magician. In 1997 she won a world title award for her 'sleight of hand' skills. She is a brilliant close-up magician.

David Blaine – a biography

David Blaine changed the way we see magic today. He took magic to the streets and made it seem cool. This is his story.

Early life

Born in Brooklyn, New York, in 1973, David Blaine came from an ordinary family. What was extraordinary was David's wish to be a magician from a very young age. He worked hard to make his dream come true by practising all the time.

Street Magic

David Blaine became famous by filming his magic with real people on the streets.

The people who saw David perform on the street could see that no special effects were used. He made people gasp with surprise by levitating and making things appear in front of their eyes. Later in this book you can learn one of David's most famous tricks – street levitation.

Death-defying stunts

David says that Houdini is his greatest inspiration. Like Houdini, he wants to perform tricks that seem to cheat death. His stunts always happen in public places. So far, he has stood on a high pillar for 34 hours, been buried alive, frozen in ice, sealed in a box for 44 days and has stayed underwater (with air) for 7 days.

Frozen in Time

Drowned Alive

How to levitate

What is levitation?

Levitation is when someone seems to rise up into the air and float. Usually, magicians use complicated props and equipment to make this happen, but this version of levitation doesn't. It's really cool because you can do it anywhere! With practice you can be a street magician – just like David Blaine!

The trick: the Balducci levitation

1. Rise up on one foot on your tiptoes.
2. Lift the other foot slowly, keeping it flat, so that it seems to float in the air.
3. Hide your supporting toes behind the front 'floating' foot.

Performing the trick

You will need your audience to stand 2–3 metres away from you. Then you should stand at a slight angle to them (about 45 degrees). This is very important because the angle you stand at hides your back foot from the audience. Slowly rise up, hover on your tiptoes and come down fast. You have levitated!

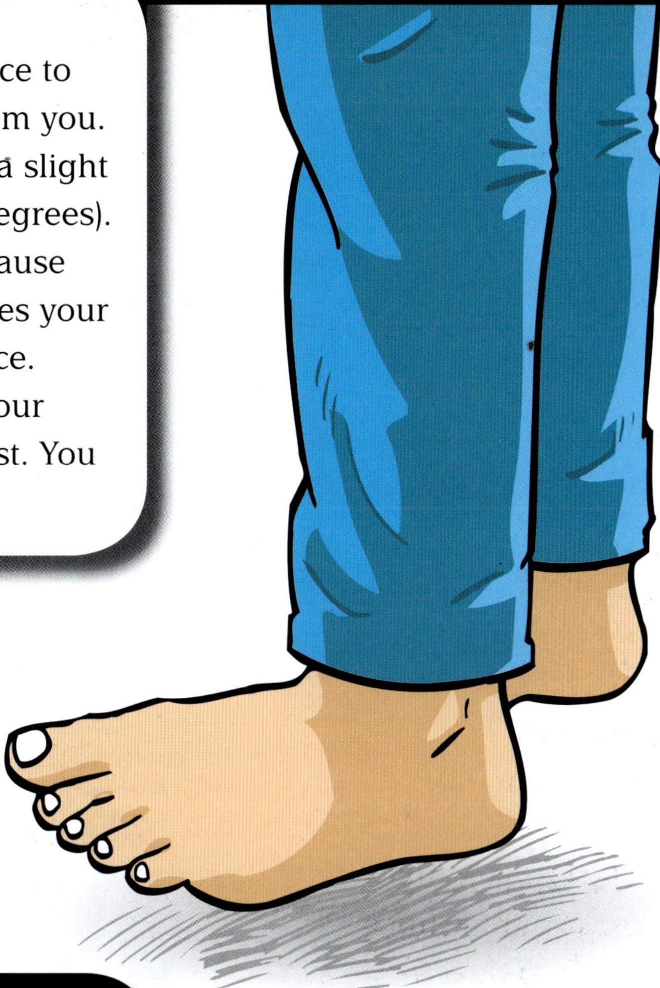

Remember – magicians practise until they have mastered the trick.

Magician's Tip

The best way to make sure your back foot is hidden is to wear trousers.

Magical dictionary

assistant *(noun)* someone who helps a magician and can be vital to the magician's **act**. He or she practises with the magician to make the tricks work smoothly.

misdirect *(verb)* the way a magician distracts the audience by making them look away so that the secret of a trick is not revealed. For example, a bird might fly out of a box just as the magician moves a card into a pocket.

patter *(noun)* the chatter of a magician while he or she performs a trick (for example, by telling a story or explaining the trick). A magician often uses patter to *misdirect* the audience.

props *(noun)* the objects used in tricks. These range from cards and coins to boxes with fake bottoms, explosions and other special effects.

sleight of hand *(noun)* how a magician uses their hands to **manipulate** objects, for example, cards, so that they appear to move magically. This is very hard and takes much practice, so sometimes magicians have to use *misdirection* as well.

A simple card trick

Two Tower Card Trick

You will need:

- a full deck of cards
- a flat surface

Before the trick
(don't let anyone see you do this!)

1. Arrange the pack of cards into two piles with the red cards in one pile and the black cards in the other. In the trick each pile will be called a 'tower'.

2. Place the two piles one on top of the other.

The trick

1. Split the deck of cards in two and put them **face** down.

2. Ask someone to choose a 'tower' and pick a card from it.

3. Then ask them to place the card into the other 'tower', anywhere they want!

4. Give them the 'tower' with their card in it and ask them to **shuffle** it. They must not look at the cards as they do so.

5. Take the 'tower' and look through it. (The chosen card is the only one which is differently coloured.)

6. Amaze your friends by showing them which card was picked.

Magician's Tip

Make sure you keep the cards face down at all times so no one sees they are all the same colour!

Three famous tricks explained

Have you ever looked at a trick and wondered – how did they do that?

Sawing a person in two

This is a famous trick and can be done in several ways. One thing is always the same – the person is never actually sawn in half!

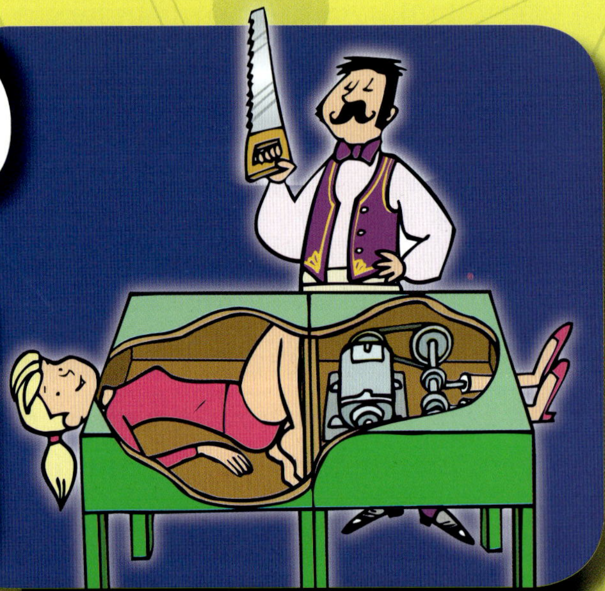

The person in the box is able to curl up in one half of it. Motor-controlled false feet stick out of the other end.

The Jigsaw is another solution. This time two people are needed, as well as a special false-bottomed box. As you can see in the diagram, the head belongs to one person, the feet another person.

Detachable thumb – The oldest magic trick?

Everybody has seen this trick and everyone can do it. Of course, your thumb does not really come off!

The finger hides the join between the two thumbs.

By moving the hands apart, the thumb appears to become detached.

Pulling a coin out of someone's ear

This is very simple.

1. Place a coin in your hand and make a fist.
2. Reach your hand behind someone's head.
3. Now move your hand slowly away from their ear. At the same time, move the coin to your fingers. The coin will appear to come out of the person's ear.

So you want to be a magician?

First read the Magician's **Oath.**

"As a magician I promise never to reveal the secret of any illusion to a non-magician, without first swearing them to the Magician's Oath. I promise never to perform any illusion for any non-magician, without first practising the effect until I can perform it well enough to maintain the illusion of magic."

Can you keep the secrets of your tricks? Will you practise until they seem like magic?

Could you be a magician?

1. When something is difficult, do you:

a. give up?

b. do something easier?

c. try again until it works?

2. Your parents ask you to clear the table. Do you:

a. tidy up one thing at a time?

b. run away?

c. stack and balance it all in the sink?

3. Your handwriting is:

a. large and spidery

b. a bit scruffy

c. neat and precise.

Mainly 'a's

Sorry, magicians need to practise, even if it's difficult.

Mainly 'b's

Magic isn't for you. Magicians need to take pride in what they do.

Mainly 'c's

You could be a magician! Magicians need steady hands, attention to detail and be able to keep on trying until they get it right.

Glossary

act – a group of tricks put together by a magician for a magic show

escapologist – someone who escapes after being tied up in some way

face – the picture side of a playing card

illusion – the performance of a trick so that it seems to be magic

Medieval – from time in history about AD 1100 – 1400

manipulate – to control or move something

oath – a promise

Index

Quiz

Find the answers in this book.

1. Who did Houdini name himself after?
2. What type of magic trick is David Blaine famous for?
3. Who entertained the Egyptian slaves?
4. Who invented the 'Chinese Water Torture' trick?
5. David Copperfield made a huge statue disappear – which one?
6. What did Dorothy Dietrich catch in her teeth?
7. How do you levitate?
8. What is the world's oldest trick?
9. Houdini was famous for what type of magic?
10. We like street magic today, but who else has enjoyed street magic?